50 Pizza Creation Recipes

By: Kelly Johnson

Table of Contents

- Margherita Pizza
- Pepperoni Pizza
- BBQ Chicken Pizza
- Hawaiian Pizza
- Veggie Supreme Pizza
- Meat Lovers Pizza
- White Pizza with Ricotta and Spinach
- Four Cheese Pizza
- Margherita with Balsamic Glaze
- Buffalo Chicken Pizza
- Pesto Chicken Pizza
- Caprese Pizza
- Mediterranean Veggie Pizza
- Philly Cheesesteak Pizza
- Prawn and Garlic Pizza
- Prosciutto and Arugula Pizza
- Truffle Mushroom Pizza
- Spicy Sausage and Peppers Pizza
- Lobster and Ricotta Pizza
- Fig and Prosciutto Pizza
- Smoked Salmon Pizza
- BBQ Pork Pizza
- Pear and Gorgonzola Pizza
- Chicken Alfredo Pizza
- Hawaiian BBQ Pizza
- Meatball Pizza
- Spicy Veggie Pizza
- Fennel Sausage Pizza
- Spaghetti Pizza
- Clam and Garlic Pizza
- Shrimp Scampi Pizza
- Zaatar and Olive Pizza
- Roasted Garlic and Herb Pizza
- Eggplant Parmesan Pizza
- Bacon and Egg Breakfast Pizza

- Chicken Parmesan Pizza
- Roasted Beet and Goat Cheese Pizza
- Sweet Potato and Sage Pizza
- Pear and Blue Cheese Pizza
- Caramelized Onion and Brie Pizza
- Shrimp and Spinach Pizza
- Mushroom and Swiss Pizza
- Spicy Mexican Pizza
- Roasted Red Pepper and Feta Pizza
- Nacho Pizza
- Peking Duck Pizza
- Shrimp and Pineapple Pizza
- Artichoke and Spinach Pizza
- Truffle and Fontina Pizza
- Lamb and Feta Pizza

Margherita Pizza

Ingredients:

- 1 pizza dough (store-bought or homemade)
- 1/2 cup tomato sauce
- 1 cup fresh mozzarella cheese, sliced
- Fresh basil leaves
- Olive oil for drizzling
- Salt and pepper to taste

Instructions:

1. Preheat the oven to 475°F (245°C).
2. Roll out the pizza dough on a lightly floured surface to your desired thickness.
3. Spread a thin layer of tomato sauce over the dough, leaving a border around the edges.
4. Arrange the mozzarella slices on top of the sauce.
5. Bake the pizza for 10-12 minutes or until the crust is golden and the cheese is melted and bubbly.
6. Remove from the oven and top with fresh basil leaves.
7. Drizzle with olive oil and season with salt and pepper before serving.

Pepperoni Pizza

Ingredients:

- 1 pizza dough
- 1/2 cup tomato sauce
- 1 cup shredded mozzarella cheese
- 1/2 cup sliced pepperoni
- Olive oil for drizzling

Instructions:

1. Preheat the oven to 475°F (245°C).
2. Roll out the pizza dough and spread the tomato sauce over the base.
3. Sprinkle the mozzarella cheese evenly over the sauce.
4. Layer the pepperoni slices over the cheese.
5. Bake for 10-12 minutes, or until the crust is golden and the cheese is bubbly and slightly browned.
6. Drizzle with olive oil before serving.

BBQ Chicken Pizza

Ingredients:

- 1 pizza dough
- 1/2 cup BBQ sauce
- 1 cup cooked chicken breast, shredded
- 1/2 red onion, thinly sliced
- 1 cup shredded mozzarella cheese
- 1/2 cup gouda cheese, shredded (optional)
- Fresh cilantro for garnish

Instructions:

1. Preheat the oven to 475°F (245°C).
2. Roll out the pizza dough and spread BBQ sauce over the base.
3. Scatter the shredded chicken and red onion over the sauce.
4. Sprinkle with mozzarella and gouda cheese.
5. Bake for 10-12 minutes, or until the crust is golden and the cheese is melted and bubbly.
6. Remove from the oven and garnish with fresh cilantro before serving.

Hawaiian Pizza

Ingredients:

- 1 pizza dough
- 1/2 cup tomato sauce
- 1 cup shredded mozzarella cheese
- 1/2 cup sliced ham
- 1/2 cup pineapple chunks (fresh or canned)
- Olive oil for drizzling

Instructions:

1. Preheat the oven to 475°F (245°C).
2. Roll out the pizza dough and spread the tomato sauce evenly over the surface.
3. Sprinkle mozzarella cheese over the sauce.
4. Add the ham and pineapple chunks.
5. Bake for 10-12 minutes, or until the crust is golden and the cheese is melted.
6. Drizzle with olive oil before serving.

Veggie Supreme Pizza

Ingredients:

- 1 pizza dough
- 1/2 cup tomato sauce
- 1 cup shredded mozzarella cheese
- 1/2 cup bell peppers, thinly sliced
- 1/2 cup red onion, thinly sliced
- 1/2 cup mushrooms, sliced
- 1/2 cup black olives, sliced
- Fresh spinach leaves
- Olive oil for drizzling

Instructions:

1. Preheat the oven to 475°F (245°C).
2. Roll out the pizza dough and spread the tomato sauce over it.
3. Sprinkle mozzarella cheese evenly on top.
4. Arrange the bell peppers, red onion, mushrooms, black olives, and spinach leaves on top of the cheese.
5. Bake for 10-12 minutes, or until the crust is golden and the cheese is melted.
6. Drizzle with olive oil before serving.

Meat Lovers Pizza

Ingredients:

- 1 pizza dough
- 1/2 cup tomato sauce
- 1 cup shredded mozzarella cheese
- 1/4 cup cooked sausage, crumbled
- 1/4 cup cooked bacon, crumbled
- 1/4 cup pepperoni slices
- 1/4 cup ham slices
- Olive oil for drizzling

Instructions:

1. Preheat the oven to 475°F (245°C).
2. Roll out the pizza dough and spread tomato sauce evenly over the surface.
3. Sprinkle mozzarella cheese on top.
4. Add the cooked sausage, bacon, pepperoni, and ham slices.
5. Bake for 10-12 minutes or until the crust is golden and the cheese is bubbly.
6. Drizzle with olive oil before serving.

White Pizza with Ricotta and Spinach

Ingredients:

- 1 pizza dough
- 1/2 cup ricotta cheese
- 1/2 cup mozzarella cheese, shredded
- 1/2 cup Parmesan cheese, grated
- 1/2 cup fresh spinach leaves
- 1 tablespoon olive oil
- 1/2 teaspoon garlic powder
- Salt and pepper to taste

Instructions:

1. Preheat the oven to 475°F (245°C).
2. Roll out the pizza dough and brush with olive oil.
3. Spread the ricotta cheese over the dough and top with mozzarella and Parmesan cheeses.
4. Add spinach leaves and sprinkle with garlic powder, salt, and pepper.
5. Bake for 10-12 minutes or until the crust is golden and the cheese is melted.
6. Drizzle with olive oil before serving.

Four Cheese Pizza

Ingredients:

- 1 pizza dough
- 1/2 cup tomato sauce
- 1/2 cup mozzarella cheese, shredded
- 1/4 cup Parmesan cheese, grated
- 1/4 cup ricotta cheese
- 1/4 cup gorgonzola cheese, crumbled
- Olive oil for drizzling

Instructions:

1. Preheat the oven to 475°F (245°C).
2. Roll out the pizza dough and spread a thin layer of tomato sauce.
3. Sprinkle the mozzarella, Parmesan, ricotta, and gorgonzola cheeses evenly on top.
4. Bake for 10-12 minutes or until the crust is golden and the cheese is bubbly.
5. Drizzle with olive oil before serving.

Margherita with Balsamic Glaze

Ingredients:

- 1 pizza dough
- 1/2 cup tomato sauce
- 1 cup fresh mozzarella cheese, sliced
- Fresh basil leaves
- Balsamic glaze for drizzling
- Olive oil for drizzling
- Salt and pepper to taste

Instructions:

1. Preheat the oven to 475°F (245°C).
2. Roll out the pizza dough and spread the tomato sauce over it.
3. Arrange the mozzarella slices on top of the sauce.
4. Bake for 10-12 minutes, or until the crust is golden and the cheese is melted.
5. Remove from the oven and top with fresh basil leaves.
6. Drizzle with balsamic glaze and olive oil. Season with salt and pepper before serving.

Buffalo Chicken Pizza

Ingredients:

- 1 pizza dough
- 1/2 cup buffalo sauce
- 1 cup cooked chicken breast, shredded
- 1 cup shredded mozzarella cheese
- 1/2 cup blue cheese crumbles
- 1/4 red onion, thinly sliced
- 1/4 cup celery, chopped (optional)
- Olive oil for drizzling

Instructions:

1. Preheat the oven to 475°F (245°C).
2. Roll out the pizza dough and spread a thin layer of buffalo sauce over it.
3. Scatter the shredded chicken over the sauce, then top with mozzarella and blue cheese crumbles.
4. Add red onion slices on top.
5. Bake for 10-12 minutes or until the crust is golden and the cheese is bubbly.
6. Once out of the oven, sprinkle with chopped celery for crunch.
7. Drizzle with olive oil before serving.

Pesto Chicken Pizza

Ingredients:

- 1 pizza dough
- 1/2 cup pesto sauce
- 1 cup cooked chicken breast, shredded
- 1/2 cup sun-dried tomatoes, sliced
- 1 cup shredded mozzarella cheese
- Olive oil for drizzling

Instructions:

1. Preheat the oven to 475°F (245°C).
2. Roll out the pizza dough and spread the pesto sauce evenly over the surface.
3. Layer the shredded chicken and sun-dried tomatoes on top.
4. Sprinkle with mozzarella cheese.
5. Bake for 10-12 minutes or until the crust is golden and the cheese is melted and bubbly.
6. Drizzle with olive oil before serving.

Caprese Pizza

Ingredients:

- 1 pizza dough
- 1/2 cup tomato sauce
- 1 cup fresh mozzarella cheese, sliced
- Fresh basil leaves
- Balsamic glaze for drizzling
- Olive oil for drizzling
- Salt and pepper to taste

Instructions:

1. Preheat the oven to 475°F (245°C).
2. Roll out the pizza dough and spread the tomato sauce over the base.
3. Arrange fresh mozzarella slices on top of the sauce.
4. Bake for 10-12 minutes or until the crust is golden and the cheese is melted.
5. Once baked, top with fresh basil leaves.
6. Drizzle with balsamic glaze and olive oil, and season with salt and pepper.

Mediterranean Veggie Pizza

Ingredients:

- 1 pizza dough
- 1/2 cup tomato sauce
- 1/2 cup green olives, sliced
- 1/2 cup Kalamata olives, sliced
- 1/2 cup artichoke hearts, sliced
- 1/2 cup red onion, thinly sliced
- 1/2 cup bell peppers, thinly sliced
- 1 cup shredded mozzarella cheese
- Olive oil for drizzling

Instructions:

1. Preheat the oven to 475°F (245°C).
2. Roll out the pizza dough and spread a thin layer of tomato sauce.
3. Add the green olives, Kalamata olives, artichoke hearts, red onion, and bell peppers on top.
4. Sprinkle with shredded mozzarella cheese.
5. Bake for 10-12 minutes or until the crust is golden and the cheese is melted.
6. Drizzle with olive oil before serving.

Philly Cheesesteak Pizza

Ingredients:

- 1 pizza dough
- 1/2 cup Alfredo sauce
- 1/2 lb thinly sliced steak (ribeye or sirloin)
- 1/2 cup bell peppers, thinly sliced
- 1/2 cup onions, thinly sliced
- 1 cup shredded mozzarella cheese
- 1/2 cup provolone cheese, shredded
- Olive oil for drizzling

Instructions:

1. Preheat the oven to 475°F (245°C).
2. Roll out the pizza dough and spread a thin layer of Alfredo sauce.
3. Sauté the bell peppers and onions in a pan until tender.
4. Layer the cooked steak, sautéed peppers, and onions over the sauce.
5. Sprinkle the mozzarella and provolone cheese on top.
6. Bake for 10-12 minutes, or until the crust is golden and the cheese is melted.
7. Drizzle with olive oil before serving.

Prawn and Garlic Pizza

Ingredients:

- 1 pizza dough
- 1/2 cup olive oil and garlic sauce (or homemade garlic butter)
- 1/2 lb prawns, peeled and deveined
- 1 cup shredded mozzarella cheese
- Fresh parsley for garnish
- Olive oil for drizzling

Instructions:

1. Preheat the oven to 475°F (245°C).
2. Roll out the pizza dough and spread a thin layer of olive oil and garlic sauce over it.
3. Arrange the prawns evenly over the sauce.
4. Sprinkle with shredded mozzarella cheese.
5. Bake for 10-12 minutes or until the crust is golden, the cheese is bubbly, and the prawns are cooked.
6. Garnish with fresh parsley and drizzle with olive oil before serving.

Prosciutto and Arugula Pizza

Ingredients:

- 1 pizza dough
- 1/2 cup tomato sauce
- 1 cup fresh mozzarella cheese, sliced
- 1/2 cup prosciutto, torn into pieces
- 1/2 cup fresh arugula
- Olive oil for drizzling

Instructions:

1. Preheat the oven to 475°F (245°C).
2. Roll out the pizza dough and spread the tomato sauce over it.
3. Arrange the mozzarella slices on top.
4. Bake for 10-12 minutes, or until the crust is golden and the cheese is melted.
5. After baking, top with prosciutto and fresh arugula.
6. Drizzle with olive oil before serving.

Truffle Mushroom Pizza

Ingredients:

- 1 pizza dough
- 1/2 cup white truffle oil
- 1/2 cup mixed mushrooms (such as cremini, shiitake, and portobello), sliced
- 1 cup shredded mozzarella cheese
- 1/2 cup Parmesan cheese, grated
- Fresh thyme for garnish
- Olive oil for drizzling

Instructions:

1. Preheat the oven to 475°F (245°C).
2. Roll out the pizza dough and brush with white truffle oil.
3. Sauté the mushrooms in a pan until tender, then layer them on the pizza.
4. Sprinkle with mozzarella and Parmesan cheese.
5. Bake for 10-12 minutes or until the crust is golden and the cheese is melted.
6. Garnish with fresh thyme and drizzle with olive oil before serving.

Spicy Sausage and Peppers Pizza

Ingredients:

- 1 pizza dough
- 1/2 cup tomato sauce
- 1/2 lb spicy Italian sausage, crumbled
- 1/2 cup bell peppers, thinly sliced
- 1/4 cup red onion, thinly sliced
- 1 cup shredded mozzarella cheese
- Olive oil for drizzling

Instructions:

1. Preheat the oven to 475°F (245°C).
2. Roll out the pizza dough and spread a thin layer of tomato sauce.
3. Cook the sausage in a pan until browned, then crumble it over the sauce.
4. Add the bell peppers and red onion on top of the sausage.
5. Sprinkle with mozzarella cheese.
6. Bake for 10-12 minutes, or until the crust is golden and the cheese is melted.
7. Drizzle with olive oil before serving.

Lobster and Ricotta Pizza

Ingredients:

- 1 pizza dough
- 1/2 cup ricotta cheese
- 1/2 cup Alfredo sauce
- 1 cup lobster meat, cooked and chopped
- 1/2 cup shredded mozzarella cheese
- 1/4 cup Parmesan cheese, grated
- Fresh parsley for garnish
- Olive oil for drizzling

Instructions:

1. Preheat the oven to 475°F (245°C).
2. Roll out the pizza dough and spread a thin layer of ricotta cheese and Alfredo sauce.
3. Scatter the lobster meat evenly over the sauce.
4. Sprinkle with mozzarella and Parmesan cheese.
5. Bake for 10-12 minutes, or until the crust is golden and the cheese is melted.
6. Garnish with fresh parsley and drizzle with olive oil before serving.

Fig and Prosciutto Pizza

Ingredients:

- 1 pizza dough
- 1/2 cup fig jam
- 1 cup fresh mozzarella cheese, sliced
- 1/2 cup prosciutto, torn into pieces
- 1/4 cup goat cheese, crumbled (optional)
- Fresh arugula
- Olive oil for drizzling

Instructions:

1. Preheat the oven to 475°F (245°C).
2. Roll out the pizza dough and spread a thin layer of fig jam over it.
3. Arrange the mozzarella slices on top.
4. Bake for 10-12 minutes, or until the crust is golden and the cheese is melted.
5. After baking, top with prosciutto, goat cheese, and fresh arugula.
6. Drizzle with olive oil before serving.

Smoked Salmon Pizza

Ingredients:

- 1 pizza dough
- 1/2 cup cream cheese, softened
- 1/4 cup sour cream
- 1 tablespoon lemon juice
- 1/2 teaspoon dill, chopped
- 1 cup smoked salmon, sliced
- 1/4 red onion, thinly sliced
- Fresh capers (optional)
- Fresh dill for garnish

Instructions:

1. Preheat the oven to 475°F (245°C).
2. Roll out the pizza dough and spread a layer of cream cheese mixed with sour cream, lemon juice, and dill.
3. Bake the pizza for 8-10 minutes, or until the crust is golden.
4. After baking, top with smoked salmon, red onion, and capers (if using).
5. Garnish with fresh dill before serving.

BBQ Pork Pizza

Ingredients:

- 1 pizza dough
- 1/2 cup BBQ sauce
- 1 cup cooked pulled pork
- 1/2 cup red onion, thinly sliced
- 1/2 cup corn kernels (optional)
- 1 cup shredded mozzarella cheese
- Fresh cilantro for garnish

Instructions:

1. Preheat the oven to 475°F (245°C).
2. Roll out the pizza dough and spread a thin layer of BBQ sauce.
3. Layer the pulled pork, red onion, and corn kernels on top.
4. Sprinkle with mozzarella cheese.
5. Bake for 10-12 minutes, or until the crust is golden and the cheese is melted.
6. Garnish with fresh cilantro before serving.

Pear and Gorgonzola Pizza

Ingredients:

- 1 pizza dough
- 1/2 cup olive oil
- 1/2 cup Gorgonzola cheese, crumbled
- 1 pear, thinly sliced
- 1/2 cup walnuts, chopped
- Fresh arugula for garnish

Instructions:

1. Preheat the oven to 475°F (245°C).
2. Roll out the pizza dough and brush with olive oil.
3. Sprinkle Gorgonzola cheese over the dough, then arrange the pear slices and chopped walnuts.
4. Bake for 10-12 minutes, or until the crust is golden and the cheese is melted.
5. Top with fresh arugula before serving.

Chicken Alfredo Pizza

Ingredients:

- 1 pizza dough
- 1/2 cup Alfredo sauce
- 1 cup cooked chicken breast, sliced
- 1/2 cup spinach, chopped
- 1 cup shredded mozzarella cheese
- Parmesan cheese, grated (optional)

Instructions:

1. Preheat the oven to 475°F (245°C).
2. Roll out the pizza dough and spread a thin layer of Alfredo sauce.
3. Layer the cooked chicken and spinach on top.
4. Sprinkle with mozzarella cheese and a little Parmesan cheese.
5. Bake for 10-12 minutes, or until the crust is golden and the cheese is melted.

Hawaiian BBQ Pizza

Ingredients:

- 1 pizza dough
- 1/2 cup BBQ sauce
- 1 cup cooked chicken breast, shredded
- 1/2 cup pineapple, diced
- 1/2 cup red onion, thinly sliced
- 1 cup shredded mozzarella cheese

Instructions:

1. Preheat the oven to 475°F (245°C).
2. Roll out the pizza dough and spread BBQ sauce over it.
3. Layer the shredded chicken, pineapple, and red onion on top.
4. Sprinkle with mozzarella cheese.
5. Bake for 10-12 minutes, or until the crust is golden and the cheese is melted.

Meatball Pizza

Ingredients:

- 1 pizza dough
- 1/2 cup marinara sauce
- 8-10 small cooked meatballs, sliced
- 1/2 cup bell peppers, thinly sliced
- 1 cup shredded mozzarella cheese
- Fresh basil for garnish

Instructions:

1. Preheat the oven to 475°F (245°C).
2. Roll out the pizza dough and spread marinara sauce over it.
3. Layer the sliced meatballs and bell peppers on top.
4. Sprinkle with mozzarella cheese.
5. Bake for 10-12 minutes, or until the crust is golden and the cheese is melted.
6. Garnish with fresh basil before serving.

Spicy Veggie Pizza

Ingredients:

- 1 pizza dough
- 1/2 cup tomato sauce
- 1/2 cup bell peppers, thinly sliced
- 1/2 cup red onion, thinly sliced
- 1/2 cup jalapeños, sliced
- 1/2 cup mushrooms, sliced
- 1 cup shredded mozzarella cheese
- 1/2 teaspoon chili flakes

Instructions:

1. Preheat the oven to 475°F (245°C).
2. Roll out the pizza dough and spread a thin layer of tomato sauce.
3. Arrange the bell peppers, red onion, jalapeños, and mushrooms over the sauce.
4. Sprinkle with mozzarella cheese and chili flakes.
5. Bake for 10-12 minutes, or until the crust is golden and the cheese is melted.

Fennel Sausage Pizza

Ingredients:

- 1 pizza dough
- 1/2 cup marinara sauce
- 1 cup fennel sausage, cooked and crumbled
- 1/2 red onion, thinly sliced
- 1/2 cup bell peppers, thinly sliced
- 1 cup shredded mozzarella cheese
- Fresh basil for garnish

Instructions:

1. Preheat the oven to 475°F (245°C).
2. Roll out the pizza dough and spread marinara sauce over it.
3. Layer the fennel sausage, red onion, and bell peppers on top.
4. Sprinkle with mozzarella cheese.
5. Bake for 10-12 minutes, or until the crust is golden and the cheese is melted.
6. Garnish with fresh basil before serving.

Spaghetti Pizza

Ingredients:

- 1 pizza dough
- 1/2 cup marinara sauce
- 1 cup cooked spaghetti, drained
- 1/2 cup meatballs, sliced
- 1 cup shredded mozzarella cheese
- 1 tablespoon Parmesan cheese, grated
- Fresh basil for garnish

Instructions:

1. Preheat the oven to 475°F (245°C).
2. Roll out the pizza dough and spread marinara sauce over it.
3. Toss the cooked spaghetti with marinara sauce, then layer it on top of the pizza.
4. Add meatball slices and sprinkle with mozzarella and Parmesan cheese.
5. Bake for 10-12 minutes, or until the crust is golden and the cheese is melted.
6. Garnish with fresh basil before serving.

Clam and Garlic Pizza

Ingredients:

- 1 pizza dough
- 2 tablespoons olive oil
- 1/2 cup garlic, minced
- 1 cup canned clams, drained
- 1/2 cup mozzarella cheese, shredded
- 1/4 cup Parmesan cheese, grated
- Fresh parsley for garnish

Instructions:

1. Preheat the oven to 475°F (245°C).
2. Roll out the pizza dough and brush with olive oil.
3. Sauté the garlic in a small pan until fragrant and spread over the pizza.
4. Layer the clams, mozzarella, and Parmesan cheese.
5. Bake for 10-12 minutes, or until the crust is golden and the cheese is melted.
6. Garnish with fresh parsley before serving.

Shrimp Scampi Pizza

Ingredients:

- 1 pizza dough
- 2 tablespoons olive oil
- 2 cloves garlic, minced
- 1 cup shrimp, peeled and deveined
- 1 tablespoon lemon juice
- 1 cup mozzarella cheese, shredded
- Fresh parsley for garnish

Instructions:

1. Preheat the oven to 475°F (245°C).
2. Roll out the pizza dough and brush with olive oil.
3. Sauté the garlic in a pan, then add shrimp and cook until pink. Add lemon juice.
4. Layer the cooked shrimp over the pizza and sprinkle with mozzarella cheese.
5. Bake for 10-12 minutes, or until the crust is golden and the cheese is melted.
6. Garnish with fresh parsley before serving.

Zaatar and Olive Pizza

Ingredients:

- 1 pizza dough
- 2 tablespoons olive oil
- 2 tablespoons za'atar seasoning
- 1/2 cup black olives, pitted and sliced
- 1/2 cup feta cheese, crumbled
- Fresh parsley for garnish

Instructions:

1. Preheat the oven to 475°F (245°C).
2. Roll out the pizza dough and brush with olive oil.
3. Sprinkle za'atar seasoning over the dough.
4. Scatter black olives and crumbled feta cheese on top.
5. Bake for 10-12 minutes, or until the crust is golden.
6. Garnish with fresh parsley before serving.

Roasted Garlic and Herb Pizza

Ingredients:

- 1 pizza dough
- 2 tablespoons olive oil
- 1/2 cup roasted garlic, mashed
- 1 tablespoon mixed herbs (oregano, thyme, rosemary)
- 1 cup mozzarella cheese, shredded
- 1/4 cup Parmesan cheese, grated

Instructions:

1. Preheat the oven to 475°F (245°C).
2. Roll out the pizza dough and brush with olive oil.
3. Spread the mashed roasted garlic over the dough.
4. Sprinkle with mixed herbs, mozzarella, and Parmesan cheese.
5. Bake for 10-12 minutes, or until the crust is golden and the cheese is melted.

Eggplant Parmesan Pizza

Ingredients:

- 1 pizza dough
- 1/2 cup marinara sauce
- 1 eggplant, sliced and roasted
- 1 cup mozzarella cheese, shredded
- 1/4 cup Parmesan cheese, grated
- Fresh basil for garnish

Instructions:

1. Preheat the oven to 475°F (245°C).
2. Roll out the pizza dough and spread marinara sauce over it.
3. Arrange the roasted eggplant slices on top.
4. Sprinkle with mozzarella and Parmesan cheese.
5. Bake for 10-12 minutes, or until the crust is golden and the cheese is melted.
6. Garnish with fresh basil before serving.

Bacon and Egg Breakfast Pizza

Ingredients:

- 1 pizza dough
- 1/2 cup cheese sauce or Alfredo sauce
- 1 cup cooked bacon, crumbled
- 2 eggs
- 1/2 cup shredded cheddar cheese
- Fresh chives for garnish

Instructions:

1. Preheat the oven to 475°F (245°C).
2. Roll out the pizza dough and spread the cheese or Alfredo sauce over it.
3. Scatter crumbled bacon over the sauce.
4. Make small wells in the pizza to crack the eggs into.
5. Sprinkle with cheddar cheese.
6. Bake for 10-12 minutes, or until the eggs are cooked and the cheese is melted.
7. Garnish with fresh chives before serving.

Chicken Parmesan Pizza

Ingredients:

- 1 pizza dough
- 1/2 cup marinara sauce
- 1 cup cooked chicken breast, sliced
- 1/2 cup mozzarella cheese, shredded
- 1/4 cup Parmesan cheese, grated
- Fresh basil for garnish

Instructions:

1. Preheat the oven to 475°F (245°C).
2. Roll out the pizza dough and spread marinara sauce over it.
3. Layer the sliced chicken breast on top.
4. Sprinkle with mozzarella and Parmesan cheese.
5. Bake for 10-12 minutes, or until the crust is golden and the cheese is melted.
6. Garnish with fresh basil before serving.

Roasted Beet and Goat Cheese Pizza

Ingredients:

- 1 pizza dough
- 2 tablespoons olive oil
- 1 cup roasted beets, sliced
- 1/2 cup goat cheese, crumbled
- 1/2 cup fresh arugula
- 1 tablespoon balsamic glaze

Instructions:

1. Preheat the oven to 475°F (245°C).
2. Roll out the pizza dough and brush with olive oil.
3. Layer the roasted beets and crumbled goat cheese on top.
4. Bake for 10-12 minutes, or until the crust is golden.
5. Top with fresh arugula and drizzle with balsamic glaze before serving.

Sweet Potato and Sage Pizza

Ingredients:

- 1 pizza dough
- 2 tablespoons olive oil
- 1 small sweet potato, peeled and thinly sliced
- 1 tablespoon fresh sage, chopped
- 1/2 cup ricotta cheese
- 1 cup mozzarella cheese, shredded
- Salt and pepper to taste
- Fresh thyme for garnish

Instructions:

1. Preheat the oven to 475°F (245°C).
2. Roll out the pizza dough and brush with olive oil.
3. Arrange the sweet potato slices over the dough in a single layer.
4. Sprinkle chopped sage, ricotta cheese, and mozzarella over the top.
5. Season with salt and pepper.
6. Bake for 10-12 minutes, or until the crust is golden and the cheese is melted.
7. Garnish with fresh thyme before serving.

Pear and Blue Cheese Pizza

Ingredients:

- 1 pizza dough
- 2 tablespoons olive oil
- 1 pear, thinly sliced
- 1/4 cup crumbled blue cheese
- 1/2 cup mozzarella cheese, shredded
- 1/4 cup walnuts, toasted and chopped
- Fresh arugula for garnish
- Honey for drizzling

Instructions:

1. Preheat the oven to 475°F (245°C).
2. Roll out the pizza dough and brush with olive oil.
3. Arrange the pear slices over the dough.
4. Sprinkle with crumbled blue cheese, mozzarella, and toasted walnuts.
5. Bake for 10-12 minutes, or until the crust is golden and the cheese is melted.
6. Garnish with fresh arugula and drizzle with honey before serving.

Caramelized Onion and Brie Pizza

Ingredients:

- 1 pizza dough
- 2 tablespoons olive oil
- 1 onion, thinly sliced
- 1 tablespoon brown sugar
- 1 tablespoon balsamic vinegar
- 1/2 cup Brie cheese, sliced
- 1/2 cup mozzarella cheese, shredded
- Fresh thyme for garnish

Instructions:

1. Preheat the oven to 475°F (245°C).
2. Roll out the pizza dough and brush with olive oil.
3. In a skillet, caramelize the onion with brown sugar and balsamic vinegar over medium heat until golden and soft.
4. Spread the caramelized onions over the pizza dough.
5. Top with Brie and mozzarella cheese.
6. Bake for 10-12 minutes, or until the crust is golden and the cheese is melted.
7. Garnish with fresh thyme before serving.

Shrimp and Spinach Pizza

Ingredients:

- 1 pizza dough
- 2 tablespoons olive oil
- 1 cup spinach, wilted
- 1 cup cooked shrimp, peeled and deveined
- 1/2 cup mozzarella cheese, shredded
- 1/4 cup Parmesan cheese, grated
- 1/2 teaspoon garlic powder
- Salt and pepper to taste

Instructions:

1. Preheat the oven to 475°F (245°C).
2. Roll out the pizza dough and brush with olive oil.
3. Spread the wilted spinach over the dough.
4. Arrange the shrimp on top and sprinkle with mozzarella and Parmesan cheese.
5. Season with garlic powder, salt, and pepper.
6. Bake for 10-12 minutes, or until the crust is golden and the cheese is melted.

Mushroom and Swiss Pizza

Ingredients:

- 1 pizza dough
- 2 tablespoons olive oil
- 1 cup mushrooms, sliced
- 1/2 cup Swiss cheese, shredded
- 1/2 cup mozzarella cheese, shredded
- 1/4 cup caramelized onions
- Fresh parsley for garnish

Instructions:

1. Preheat the oven to 475°F (245°C).
2. Roll out the pizza dough and brush with olive oil.
3. Spread the caramelized onions over the dough.
4. Add the sliced mushrooms and top with Swiss and mozzarella cheese.
5. Bake for 10-12 minutes, or until the crust is golden and the cheese is melted.
6. Garnish with fresh parsley before serving.

Spicy Mexican Pizza

Ingredients:

- 1 pizza dough
- 1/2 cup salsa
- 1/2 cup cooked ground beef or chicken
- 1/2 cup black beans, drained and rinsed
- 1 cup shredded cheddar cheese
- 1/4 cup jalapeño slices
- 1/4 cup red onion, thinly sliced
- Fresh cilantro for garnish
- Sour cream for serving

Instructions:

1. Preheat the oven to 475°F (245°C).
2. Roll out the pizza dough and spread salsa over it.
3. Layer the ground meat, black beans, cheddar cheese, jalapeños, and red onions.
4. Bake for 10-12 minutes, or until the crust is golden and the cheese is melted.
5. Garnish with fresh cilantro and serve with a dollop of sour cream.

Roasted Red Pepper and Feta Pizza

Ingredients:

- 1 pizza dough
- 2 tablespoons olive oil
- 1/2 cup roasted red peppers, sliced
- 1/4 cup crumbled feta cheese
- 1/2 cup mozzarella cheese, shredded
- 1/4 cup kalamata olives, pitted and sliced
- Fresh oregano for garnish

Instructions:

1. Preheat the oven to 475°F (245°C).
2. Roll out the pizza dough and brush with olive oil.
3. Arrange the roasted red pepper slices over the dough.
4. Sprinkle with feta cheese, mozzarella, and kalamata olives.
5. Bake for 10-12 minutes, or until the crust is golden and the cheese is melted.
6. Garnish with fresh oregano before serving.

Nacho Pizza

Ingredients:

- 1 pizza dough
- 1/2 cup salsa
- 1 cup seasoned ground beef or chicken
- 1/2 cup black beans, drained and rinsed
- 1 cup shredded cheddar cheese
- 1/2 cup tortilla chips, crushed
- 1/4 cup diced tomatoes
- 1/4 cup sliced jalapeños
- Sour cream for serving
- Fresh cilantro for garnish

Instructions:

1. Preheat the oven to 475°F (245°C).
2. Roll out the pizza dough and spread salsa evenly over it.
3. Layer the seasoned ground beef or chicken, black beans, cheddar cheese, and crushed tortilla chips on top.
4. Add diced tomatoes and jalapeños.
5. Bake for 10-12 minutes, or until the crust is golden and the cheese is melted.
6. Garnish with fresh cilantro and serve with a dollop of sour cream.

Peking Duck Pizza

Ingredients:

- 1 pizza dough
- 2 tablespoons hoisin sauce
- 1/2 cup cooked duck breast, thinly sliced
- 1/4 cup scallions, thinly sliced
- 1/2 cup shredded mozzarella cheese
- 1/4 cup cilantro leaves
- 1 tablespoon sesame seeds

Instructions:

1. Preheat the oven to 475°F (245°C).
2. Roll out the pizza dough and spread hoisin sauce evenly over it.
3. Arrange the sliced duck breast on top of the sauce.
4. Sprinkle with scallions, mozzarella, and sesame seeds.
5. Bake for 10-12 minutes, or until the crust is golden and the cheese is melted.
6. Garnish with fresh cilantro leaves before serving.

Shrimp and Pineapple Pizza

Ingredients:

- 1 pizza dough
- 2 tablespoons olive oil
- 1/2 cup cooked shrimp, peeled and deveined
- 1/2 cup pineapple, diced
- 1/2 cup mozzarella cheese, shredded
- 1/4 cup red onion, thinly sliced
- Fresh cilantro for garnish

Instructions:

1. Preheat the oven to 475°F (245°C).
2. Roll out the pizza dough and brush with olive oil.
3. Arrange the shrimp, pineapple, and red onion over the dough.
4. Sprinkle with mozzarella cheese.
5. Bake for 10-12 minutes, or until the crust is golden and the cheese is melted.
6. Garnish with fresh cilantro before serving.

Artichoke and Spinach Pizza

Ingredients:

- 1 pizza dough
- 1/2 cup cream cheese, softened
- 1/2 cup cooked spinach, drained
- 1/2 cup marinated artichoke hearts, chopped
- 1/2 cup mozzarella cheese, shredded
- 1/4 cup Parmesan cheese, grated
- Fresh garlic for garnish

Instructions:

1. Preheat the oven to 475°F (245°C).
2. Roll out the pizza dough and spread cream cheese evenly over it.
3. Top with cooked spinach, chopped artichokes, mozzarella, and Parmesan cheese.
4. Bake for 10-12 minutes, or until the crust is golden and the cheese is melted.
5. Garnish with fresh garlic before serving.

Truffle and Fontina Pizza

Ingredients:

- 1 pizza dough
- 2 tablespoons olive oil
- 1/2 cup Fontina cheese, shredded
- 1/2 cup mozzarella cheese, shredded
- 1 tablespoon truffle oil
- Fresh arugula for garnish
- Fresh cracked black pepper for garnish

Instructions:

1. Preheat the oven to 475°F (245°C).
2. Roll out the pizza dough and brush with olive oil.
3. Sprinkle Fontina and mozzarella cheese over the dough.
4. Drizzle truffle oil on top.
5. Bake for 10-12 minutes, or until the crust is golden and the cheese is melted.
6. Garnish with fresh arugula and cracked black pepper before serving.

Lamb and Feta Pizza

Ingredients:

- 1 pizza dough
- 2 tablespoons olive oil
- 1/2 cup cooked lamb, thinly sliced
- 1/4 cup feta cheese, crumbled
- 1/2 cup red onion, thinly sliced
- 1/4 cup fresh mint leaves
- 1/4 cup tzatziki sauce for serving

Instructions:

1. Preheat the oven to 475°F (245°C).
2. Roll out the pizza dough and brush with olive oil.
3. Arrange the sliced lamb, crumbled feta, and red onion over the dough.
4. Bake for 10-12 minutes, or until the crust is golden and the cheese is melted.
5. Garnish with fresh mint leaves and serve with tzatziki sauce.

www.ingramcontent.com/pod-product-compliance
Lightning Source LLC
LaVergne TN
LVHW081343060526
838201LV00055B/2819